Husbandry:

an ancient art for the modern world

Jonty Williams

The Husbandry School

Henry George Society of Devon

Published by   **Lulu**.com

First published 23rd May 2014
ISBN   978-1-291-88757-0

To order a paperback copy go to www.lulu.com
A (free) pdf download is available from:
www.husbandry.co.uk/downloads and from
http://henrygeorgedevon.wordpress.com/

Cover picture. The cover picture consists of a felt image of piece of the earth by Carole Williams, wife to land at Liddy Ball, bounded by re-used baler twine plaited by Walter Edwards, husband to land at Fair Oak.

Acknowledgements. The author would like to thank:

Julian Pratt (www.stewardship.ac) for his editorial skill and persistent encouragement.

Jane MacNamee (www.jmeditorialservices.co.uk) for working a miracle and turning my words into English.

Marcus Fernée, fellow earth-user, for the title.

The Edwards family of Upottery for husbandry teachings, deep gratitude.

and above all my amazing wife Carole for her love and trust during all the (excessive!) time this has taken.

I am very grateful to Mr Wendell Berry for his kind encouragement and assurance that my quotation from his essay is 'fair use'.

For Carole

(husband to wife), with love

CONTENTS

A hundred years ago both my grandfathers, Alfred and Arthur, were young men, the same sort of age as my sons and daughter are now. The Titanic had just sunk. The gross indignities of obscene decadence, poverty and corruption were right in front of their eyes ... and are now right in front ours...

We seem to be following in the footsteps of those young men in the early years of the 20th century. It was just a year away from the start of the terrible First World War. My grandfathers and grandmothers must have had the same queasy feelings that we are having. Today, there are big forces at work and they are not looking like they are taking us in any good direction. There seems to be a systemic flaw at the heart of humanity's interaction with our planet.

How many of us feel that our problems this time are not going to be patched up in the time-honoured fashion of analysing the cause of each problem and solving it with a new sticking plaster or even a war?

Handling the Dirt – and Cleaning Up After

Picture the scene. It is January. The sheep and I are huddled in an outside pen, half on concrete, half on hay-strewn mud, next to the goats which are in two inside pens – four-star accommodation in comparison – deeply-bedded on dry fresh smelling hay. There is even a waft of summer haymeadow in the night-time sleet right now.

Nearly all the sheep's feet need attention. They have walked around on soggy pastures for the last nine months, barring that brief haymaking week, last July. Each hoof grows without being worn down. The softened horn on the edge splits away from the pad. Mud and dirt gather in the gap and a sore patch forms. A certain pair of bacteria help each other to the nutrient mix made up of sore hoof and rotting sheep muck [1].

---

[1] Fusobacterium necrophorum and Bacteroides melaninogenicus
http://en.wikipedia.org/wiki/Foot_rot

The sheep are just in lamb – the ram went in on bonfire night accompanied by fireworks and he, together with his forty-nine ewes, have been enjoying each others' company ever since.

My task is to trim off the split horn, as carefully and completely as possible, and spray the wounds with stuff the bacteria won't like. Then, with electric shears, I cut the dirty wool from the sheeps' backsides. The sheep are wet, we are all wet, the foot trimming shears, as sharp as possible, are slippery in my hands and the sheep struggle.

The sheep, the whole hilltop, me, my amazing wife, the barn, our house, the whole land is wet. The ducks and the earthworms, the hoof and horn, the concrete, the bedding hay, are all wet. We people, plants, soil and animals are wet.

YET … we are a 'we'. We are in this together. We have a 'belonging' – sheep, shears, concrete, wet pen, people, stars, sleet, pairs of bacteria, the spray to control them, husband and wife, hilltop; all dwelling, growing and decaying in, on, over and under it.

It is this sense of community that embraces stones, water and soil that Aldo Leopold was talking about when he said, "We abuse land because we see it as a commodity belonging to us. When we see land as a community to which we belong, we may begin to use it with love and respect" [2].

On this dark winter's night I feel this belonging strongly. The reality of land as a community sinks home when it becomes felt. This is an earth community to which I belong.

This mutual belonging – this settling on a future in intimate relationship with a geographically located ecological, social and economic community – is the story of humanity. Each person, each people, each place with its special perspective has myriad stories both of the amazing – and the tragic – to tell.

---

[2] Aldo Leopold, A Sand County Almanac 1948 page viii

An understanding of this mutual belonging, it seems to me, is needed for humanity and our world to see the way out of the mess we are making for ourselves. Particularly, we need to reassess the part played in the 'belonging' by us human members of the 'we': the role represented by the *husband* and *wife*. We are the two 'alphas' of this small hilltop. We also need to reassess the alpha role represented by those above us, the power of state and corporate institutions. It seems to me that it is like a beast we humans have released and it is becoming obvious to everyone that it needs taming.

I will leave to my beautiful and skilful wife a telling of the – to me totally magic – role of the woman in the 'we'. Just as there is a long tradition of teaching the skills and philosophy of husbandry here in Devon (we will come to that later), so also there is a long tradition of teaching the skills and philosophy of *hus-wifery*. If feminism has taught us anything it is that men can learn from the traditions of womancraft and vice versa.

To understand from the husband's point of view we must proceed with the foot trimming and "dagging" (trimming the bums). After Rameses the ram, Apache the lead sheep and the other breeding sheep are done, there is quite a mess on the concrete. The bedding is dunged and trodden, there is an accumulation of trimmed dirty wool mixed with too many smelly and bloody hoof clippings and the concrete needs mucking out.

Each time I clean the concrete I am taken back to my first day working for my husbandry teacher Walter. He had a very, very strong belonging with his land, his sheep, his cows and his concrete yards. The land he belonged to was called Fair Oak. He belonged to the dung and daggings of Fair Oak's ecologies, just as he belonged to the banks, fields, oak woods and magnificent landscapes that were also Fair Oak's ecologies. It was my first task as junior of the juniors of apprentices, to shovel and sweep the cow shit after milking that morning. Walter gave me that job, I now see, as the most important job. The one highest in the hierarchy of humanity's tasks – the handling of the dirt.

Part one of the job is to stack it neatly. This is valuable stuff. It is the driver of the *katabolic metabolism* of the land's ecology. This mixture of hay, sleet, mud, sheep shit, goat shit, foot-rotten parings, all needs handling. It is the job of the husband to handle the dirt. The next step is to find the best place for the muck.

Mine is for it to go to the hayfields – it is full of grass, clover, vetch and wild flower seeds gathered with the hay last July. Hayfields need to be fenced to control grazing and let the grass grow long. Ground belonging to the husband and his shit needs to be fenced.

Noah's trade

At this point we need to introduce the concept of husbandry – or rather reintroduce it – because in old usage the word 'husbandry' described the art of managing the human-to-land relationship. Let's look at its pedigree so that we have an idea of what help the concept could give us today, and in the coming years.

It has a long tradition, first mentioned, as far as I have been able to find out, in the early chapters of Genesis, when Noah became a 'husbandman' – (The bible goes on to say the first thing he did when he began to practise husbandry was to plant a vineyard, get drunk on the wine and then wake up to find himself naked and exposed in his tent …but that is another story) [3].

Those early scriptures also defined this art – this occupation that Noah realised was his true calling – as 'earth-man' or 'earth-human': the Greek word used in early texts was γεωργια or *georgia* [4] which literally means 'earth-urger' and the Hebrew used was *Adama-Ish* or *ish haadamah* [5] which

[3] Genesis chapter 9 verse 20

[4] Works of Philo Judaeus, *On Husbandry*
  http://www.earlychristianwritings.com/yonge/book11.html

[5] http://www.sacred-texts.com/bib/cmt/clarke/gen009.htm

means 'earth-person' – one who 'looked after' the earth as well as one 'made of' the earth.

Here is a definition of husbandry from an essay called *Renewing Husbandry* written by Wendell Berry:

> "To husband is to use with care, to keep, to save, to make last, to conserve. Old usage tells us that beyond the household there is a husbandry of the land, of the soil, of the domestic plants and animals – obviously because of the importance of these things to the household. And there have been times, one of which is now, when some people have tried to think of a proper human husbandry of the nondomestic creatures. One reason for this is the dependence of our households and domestic life upon the wild world.
>
> Husbandry is the name of all the practices that sustain life by connecting us conservingly to our places and our world, the art of keeping tied all the strands in the living network that sustains us" [6].

A few other translations of Husbandry are *Haus-halten, Agricultura, Economie, Administrioni,* and the old English word Yeomanry (from *yo,* old European for the earth) [7].

So, this is an ancient art, and yet the word is known now only in its very rudimentary and narrow meaning of animal husbandry – the looking after of animals.

Tracing its story through the evolution of English, we come across it used to describe 'economy' [8] - the art of the relationship with our domestic dwelling places - and this brings us to its literal meaning. Its etymological roots are from *hus,* old European for a dwelling place and 'band' or 'bond' meaning a relationship, like a marriage bond, and also a place of boundary – the meeting point between the

---

[6] http://faculty.washington.edu/stevehar/Berry%20Husbandry.pdf page 3

[7] http://translate.google.com/#en/cy/husbandry

[8] Definition from A New English Dictionary on Historical Principles 1897

practitioner of husbandry and the land within which he or she finds themselves [9].

When we use the word as a verb we may talk about 'husbanding' the earthly resources we find ourselves surrounded by. This bond between human and land is one of husband married, with intimacy, emotion, even love, to the particular places of the world we find ourselves in.

Further on we find husbandry referred to by Shakespeare as a thing that may be damaged by borrowing, just as lending may lose us both what we lend and the friend we lend to:

> "Never a lender nor a borrower be,
>
> For loan oft losses both itself and friend
>
> And borrowing dulls the edge of husbandry" [10]

Is the point that Shakespeare is making that by borrowing you can dodge the full responsibility of husbandry?

Later in the 1700s we hear of husbandry referred to as "the first and most useful of all the necessary arts" [11]. This comes from a wonderful book on how the early civilisations conducted (and failed to conduct) their relationship with the land. The book, *Husbandry of the Ancients,* is by a Scottish gentleman called Adam Dickson.

In the 18th and 19th centuries we find mention of husbandry in legal documents, and here we come to my personal story of how this important art came to my notice.

In the spring of 2003 my husbandry teacher, Walter, died. In dealing with my grief at his death and wanting to let others know about the life of this great man, I found myself searching through old papers relating to his farm in the local archives. I found some interesting documents.

---

[9] A New English Dictionary on Historical Principles, 1897 pages 471 to 473

[10] Hamlet Act 1, scene 3

[11] Adam Dickson, Husbandry of the Ancients 1788 vol 1 page xii

I found husbandry referred to in an agricultural lease (1722)[12] where Ann Rogers, a tenant of Faire Oak, was legally bound to practise various methods of "good husbandry" on the land she occupied.

I also found husbandry referred to in an apprentice document, dated 1742, as a trade that was required to be "taught and instructed"[13]. The teacher of this trade was the same Ann Rogers and the period of training (an Indentured Labour term) was for fourteen years. The pupil, ten year old "poor boy of the parish" called John Pooke, would have ended up a highly-skilled young man when he was given his freedom – together with two suits of new clothes, one for working days and one for holy days – at the age of twenty four. The skilled trade he had acquired was called husbandry.

I worked alongside Walter for five years in the 1970s. He and his family have always showed me the best of Devon hospitality. He was as good, strong and as intelligent a man as I have ever met. He also had as strong and tenacious a love for his land as I have ever seen in anyone. As for me, unfortunately, like many an arrogant young man, I thought I knew too soon what I was being taught. It is only now, ten years after his death, that I consider I have completed my full fourteen years of apprenticeship in the business of husbandry and have the earned the privilege of carrying out my journey in the trade. I now understand that this trade, this art, informs every aspect of my connections with the land and its communities that I am a member of. It is the art of learning to take care.

There are so many levels to learn. Learning proper boundaries of hospitality towards the stuff of the world is so urgently needed. Unfortunately, I am a poor learner. I am a

---

[12] This lease is available to view in the Exeter Records office in the papers of the Viscounts Sidmouth. A transcription of it is here: http://www.husbandry.co.uk/indenture.html

[13] Also available to view at Exeter Records office Apprentice Indenture 1742, copy available at http://www.husbandry.co.uk/index.html

poor husband, and a poor husbander. We humans are all poor learners, but, nevertheless, learners we are. We must begin from where we are.

So now this story of husbandry of the land – the big picture how-to-dos for humanity – has hard evidence for its place at the centre of the cultural traditions of English speaking peoples. Here in Devon this subject is still being taught. It very nearly died out, all traces lost and forgotten ... there are just a few lone voices calling for a renewal of husbandry.

Conflict and Resolution: the task of aligning economic motivation with the care of the land and its communities.

So, some dirt is handled, and now, after much washing, I have clean hands. The latex gloves helped a lot and the scars are healing.

Let us diverge a little from the agrarian to the urban. It is still January. I am in London writing this. There are so many places and so many people surrounding me, each telling stories of the amazing and of the tragic. I walked along Oxford Street today. It tells one story and another and another... Endless stories of the amazing and the tragic are in all the faces of the people surrounding me. I see a 'wanting to behave fairly' overriding all else.

The facade of Selfridges, the detail in the stone carvings on the columns and friezes matches the Parthenon in its intricacy. This is just one example from the time of my grandfathers' youth of the heights urban culture can reach. This urban art is what we usually call 'high culture'. All the arts, architecture, music and theatre here in the West End, the 3D cinema pictures around the corner in Leicester Square, the gilded sculptures, high on the street corners, all demonstrate deep-felt emotions.

I fear that all this culture will be effectively rendered ephemeral, transient, only to be here a moment and then destroyed, if we, urban humans, neglect "the first and most useful of all the necessary arts".

Those sheep's feet trace their story way, way back in the human story of this part of the world. Thousands upon thousands of years ago ways of hunting evolved into a managed belonging: shepherd to sheep, sheep to shepherd. The sheep's pasture became a 'belonging' – a fenced-off hayfield became a 'belonging'. This land and people belonging is where conflict over land as property arises. The Cain and Abel story in Genesis [14] is about a nomadic herder and a settler, and their difference of opinion about the nature of belonging to land. This is an archetypal conflict – and it is a conflict over land. In the story, Cain, a herder, becomes jealous of Abel, a settled tiller of the earth, and murders him. Cain's punishment is never to be allowed to settle… The way a wanderer belongs conflicts with the way a settler belongs…

So, as we have seen, if a settled farmer is to become a proper member of a land community, to have somewhere productive to tend with tenderness to the fertility of hayfields or vineyards, then a boundary needs to be constructed. This enables the vines or the hay to grow ungrazed by some passing wild beasts. However it is this act of enclosure that gives rise to conflict. Hayfield boundaries are backed up with force.

This Cain and Abel conflict, this armed and forcible protection of fenced lands – together with the wonderful nurturing of beauty, wealth and ever cleverer manipulation of nature possible within and outside fences – has become the story of humanity. The tragedy of the conflict of who and how we belong to the land and how the land belongs to us has been the constant travelling companion of all of us humans ever since we have been humans.

The conflict between the *settler* and her need for secure lifelong tenure of her hayfields and vineyards and the *wanderer* of the big ecologies and her deprivation of places to nourish *her* communities is behind all these stories of both amazing and tragic humanity evident in the city.

---

[14] Genesis chapter IV verse 2

Perhaps this can help us in our quest to find the systemic flaw in the human-to-planet relationship...

Let me state clearly once again what this conflict is about. The settler needs exclusive use of his homestead in order to practise the stewardship of the communities in the land that he sees himself a member of. The settler needs some sort of long-term secure tenure in order to conduct this relationship. The wanderers, on the other hand, together with all other potential users of that patch of land are deprived of their right and responsibility to steward, to husband and to form any attachment, emotional or otherwise, to that part of the Earth. They are deprived of that use for the whole length of the settler's tenure of the land. There is no compensation available to them. The bottom line is that they are kept out by force.

Approaches to Resolution

We in our long history and prehistory seem to have tried every which way to resolve this conflict. We have tried smashing rocks at each other's heads, firing artillery shells and machine guns at each other in trenches; we have tried every sneaky, surreptitious and cheating way of felling the monster we have grown out of this age-old and *real* Cain and Abel conflict.

We have also tried setting up organising power structures based on the teachings that nature has shown to a few perceptive ones. Those few perceptive ones have seen that a violent approach is no good way to coax the best out of a relationship with nature – whether it is a sheep, the dirt, or whether it is my neighbour, settler or wanderer.

Many, many attempts have been made in and between every culture the world over to resolve this problem.

Here are just a few examples:

There was an early middle-eastern Jubilee tradition [15] which was a returning to a more sharing relationship

---

[15] Michael Hudson, The lost tradition of biblical debt cancellations 1993

between people and their lands once in every forty-nine years or on the change of the ruling monarch. The Jubilee was a redistribution of lands and a writing-off of debts accumulated on the collateral of lands, and has much to recommend it as a route out of our current debt crisis. (Come on Queen Elizabeth and Prince Charles: time to meet your deep rooted constitutional obligation to real/royal estate and bring on a proper jubilee!)

Then there were the Romans – the early Roman Republic before they allowed greed, that is. They enacted a first Agrarian Law [16]. Each Roman citizen, including all the senators and generals, cultivated the land. So that the land was well looked after and the work of nature well respected, each citizen was required to fence off no more than 2 *Jugera* or about 1.2 acres of land. In these productive gardens they grew the crops they needed. The wheat for their bread, the linseed for their togas, fishing nets and sails, willow with roots in the wet bits was grown for vines with roots in well-drained bits to climb up. These must have been truly productive gardens and are well described by the classical writers gathered together in Adam Dickson's wonderful volumes of *Husbandry of the Ancients*.

Then a second Agrarian Law came about after a short few centuries and 7 acres was allowed. Then a third - 50 acres was the rule – then as Roman power became addictive, if you fought for the Roman army you would be allotted stretches of land determined only by your military prowess.

The land came to be seen, in this progression, as a thing to be owned, and this included all the ecological communities the land contained, including the people in it. The logic of the thing says that if I can 'own' a fenced-off 1.2 acre garden including all the ecologies in it, I can own a huge estate with all its inhabitants on their patches of land. The slavery of humans and the slavery of land have much in common.

---

[16] Adam Dickson Husbandry of the Ancients 1788 vol 1 page 6

Boundaries of Hospitality

The problem, once again, is to resolve the conflict between exclusive settled use of land and the denial of use of this land to those excluded.

We come now to the key link. The link is between the payment of rent for exclusive use of land and its use to compensate the landless. One way of compensating the landless is for the state to use land rent to provide common goods. This is what Adam Smith saw in *The Wealth of Nations*: that ways to fund public affairs from ground 'rent' lay at the heart of seeking justice out of the human relationship with land [17].

Henry George [18] was an American philosopher and political economist who wrote a very influential work in 1879 called *Progress and Poverty*. He and his followers – great respected thinkers like Leo Tolstoy [19], Winston Churchill [20], Albert Einstein and SunYat Sen – came very close to resolving our problem a hundred or so years ago. George had a clear understanding that the magnitude of the fight over the fences on land was an indicator of the value, to both sides of the fence, of the deal that needs to be struck for dignity to be restored in the land conflict.

George's proposal was that a market value, the rental value of location, should be paid as a 'user fee' by the user for the right to exclusive use of a location. This fee was to be paid to the existing recognised jurisdiction as the proper and *only* funding the jurisdiction needed. This user fee is a payment of proper dues, and serves to compensate society for being excluded from using the piece of the earth that has become private property. He proposed what he called a Single Tax, i.e. that *no* payments should be made by the handlers of the

[17] Adam Smith, The Wealth of Nations, book V chapter 2 article 1: Taxes upon the Rent of Houses 1776

[18] Henry George, Progress and Poverty 1879

[19] David Redfearn, Tolstoy: Principles for a New World Order 1992

[20] Winston Churchill on Land monopoly: www.landvaluetax.org/current-affairs-comment/winston-churchill-said-it-all-better-then-we-can.html

dirt – the husbandmen – *other* than this location rent. This would be the sole means of raising revenue for the civil authorities to provide for the protection and enjoyment of the jurisdiction's laws, and all other public services. George realised that the value of any location was generated by the community gathered in that location and this value should therefore rightly belong to the community for community use, and not be appropriated through the system of land ownership which had inadvertently grown around the need for husbanders of nature to have secure tenure. George's proposal had the advantage that a simple fiscal adjustment to the means of raising public revenue was all that was needed for economic justice to be achieved; no revolution was required.

However, since then we have had a diminishing understanding of the way towards a remedy for the sorts of surreptitious and overt violence that has lasted all the way from Cain and Abel through to today. For so long we have had an economy under which it makes sense to give up on husbandry.

Husbandry of the holistic ecologies, husbandry of the complex connections associated with a deep understanding of land, has long been given up on. Success in agriculture, industry, and business of every sort under our existing systems can only be achieved by giving up on husbandry, by losing the word from our language and forgetting even the possibility of holistic relationships with the soil.

To put this right comes down to us: me and you and you – us – we. The 'us' and 'we' communities – wanderer, settler or both – there are centuries of stories to tell of ways that work and ways that don't. These combinations of human communities and ecologies which form the cultures of the world, have evolved clever, time-honoured ways of doing husbandry. We may have to search hard for these ways but they exist at the heart of all communities.

Each small part of the inhabited physical world has an ancient past, linked to some human culture, and every one of us humans alive today has ancient links to cultural practices that have proven successful over the thousands of years of our ancestry. We are all linked, both genetically and culturally, to all the multitudes of places on the planet and to systems of husbandry that have proven themselves over thousands of years.

What each and every one of us has to do is start to look after a piece of ground – any piece, including its boundaries – and begin the journey of belonging.

There are stories, like the one I discovered on the farm I worked, about the connections to land and the proper traditions of these connections. There are stories which originate in every place, told today by storytellers all over the world, which link all the various cultures of humanity with all these places on the earth we inhabit. These stories are our guide.

Husbandry, we must not forget, is an ever creative art – the art of the human in the human-to-land marriage. We people, and our mutual leadership, are the only hope.

We can begin to protect our boundaries in an hospitable and civilised way. We do not need to threaten our neighbours, who might want what we belong to, with terrible weapons.

Husbandry's Edge

What can we do? Is there a framework to help us align the economic forces we are all subjected to with the task of beginning to learn about the levels of taking care of the bounded parcels of our world? The careful tiny increments of effort, emotion, love and skill which bring fertility and the growth of good things, has had to be lost in the rush to economic growth needed to compete in the system of usury of the world's resources we are suffering under in the modern world.

"Borrowing dulls the edge of husbandry". I had not before now considered husbandry had an edge.

The hay is nearly ready for cutting. I have been using tools in the garden today: my mattock, my spade, my wheelbarrow, fork and rake. The season has now gone all the way through spring to a fine June day. The first two tools are to cut the horizontal and the vertical cuts in turf to define the boundaries between grass and other crops. I sharpened them on a grindstone and resharpened them a few times during today and yesterday. The edge makes such a difference to the ease of the job. The edges of my mattock and my spade are now bright. What is it that we need to do to brighten the edge of husbandry? What is it that we need to do to give husbandry the edge over usury?

Henry George and many others following him today have pointed out a possible way. Their particular insight was the separation of the value of nature enclosed from the wealth generated by the encloser. The right justice lies not in depriving a person of any of the manifestations of their effort, whether it be a wet concrete sheep yard or the Selfridges building – whether it be a weapon or any other tool of any other trade. The right justice lies in having no taxes *at all*. Taxes are all theft of the products of our efforts. Taxes mean that small, incremental improvements, like the addition of foot trimmings to the fertility of a hayfield are uneconomic and therefore prohibited by the system we all operate under. Taxes need to all be abolished along with all the debts heaped on land that "dulls the husbandry" of it all. The right justice lies instead in sharing the value of the locations of nature enclosed throughout the communities which create that value.

I am a settler. I want to pay you enough for you to feel properly compensated.

The question is this:

How much is it worth to you, dear traveller, dear neighbour, – for me as husbander of this enclosure, to deprive you of your use of it? I'll pay you annually or monthly or whenever, but I want to be able to feel secure in my life time here in my wet and bloody, yet loving, relationship with my soil.

I want to pay my dues so I have legitimate right to be here. How much should I pay?

I want to feel secure in a dignified and respectful relationship with all of you who are excluded from this land by my tenure of it. I know my security will only be achieved when you are secure. You need full compensation so that my boundaries can be seen to show hospitality.

So, the question is this: how much do I pay you for my hilltop acres, or how much does the landlord responsible for the husbandry of the location of Selfridges – No. 400 Oxford Street – pay for that, oh so much more valuable, location?

Mine, I can tell you pretty accurately. We have a farm business tenancy on some steep fields at our Husbandry School. This is the ground where the sheep and the goats mostly graze and browse. We pay just over £50 an acre per year for this grazing and browsing grade 5 land. (The scale goes from 1 to 5, one being best land). This is the going agricultural rate, as valued by the highly esteemed valuers, Sawdye and Harris, our local auctioneers. These values are based on regular auctions for seasonal rented land. Our freehold land is adjacent to this and so the annual rental value of it will be in this ball park.

The location of Selfridges has a somewhat different value. Not tens of pounds per year, but millions. It is so much more because London yields so much more wealth. London yields so much more wealth because so many people want to be there to do their business. This amount is paid at present ultimately to the freeholder (or long leaseholder) of that location. Whoever holds those title deeds at present receives that location rent. If loans are secured on the land title, then most probably it is the bank which holds these title deeds. Whether it is in the hands of the long standing aristocratic establishment, or in the hands of a fly-by-night bank, its value maintains the power base of London. This value is literally the grounding of the power base of London. This is one side of land use – the location.

The other side of land use is our tenure of it – our physical daily use of the real stuff of the world we need to handle to give us our living. It is my opinion that all forms of tenure need to have husbandry clauses, just like the ones they have

16

on agricultural leases in Devon. I believe these are even more vitally important for tenure of the more valuable locations such as the busy cities. Just as the realisation that the people attached to land may not be owned and that slavery is an affront to our humanity, so too the ownership of the ecologies of our fields and streets is an affront to our humanity. The traditions of love, respect and dignified dealings inherent in all the many husbandry traditions around the world need to be brought into occupancy rights to land.

This distinction between ownership and stewardship is clearly set out by my friend, Julian Pratt, in his important book *Stewardship Economy: private property without private ownership* [21].

Husbandry is a personal thing – it is an art growing and spiralling with each person carrying on with it. We are continually learning about handling the dirt in ways that allow our hands to be cleaned. We are learning about respecting the dirt just as much as the cleanliness. It is personal to places and people. This human-to-earth relationship is the cellular structure of culture. It is that relationship which large-scale civic debate has all but lost.

Right now is the time to reclaim it. People the world over are realising that looking after a small bounded piece of the earth with respect and dignity is a good way out of this mess. We are learning to grow something useful out of something disregarded. The cellular structures of intimacy, between people and patches of land, are the building blocks of the earth's cultures.

So, we are still back at that essential human conundrum...

Our humanity desires an honouring, dignified relationship with the ecologies we live alongside. For this to occur we need a peaceable substrate. We need long enough, secure enough tenure of all the various locations we would like to inhabit to enable the slow feedback of love for the land to

---

[21] Julian Pratt, Stewardship Economy 2011

grow. A lifetime's tenure would be just about right. ("Three lives" tenancies is also a tradition in here in Devon [22]. Devon is a place famous for its respect for fair dealings.) We need to resharpen the dulled edge of husbandry.

This is where the 'we' comes in: your particular 'we' and mine. The soils beneath where your feet most like to tread are included in your 'we' and mine – 'we' as members of land communities – me with my 'we' and you with yours, overlapping.

Unwittingly looking up to the big powerful players as the alphas from whom to expect salvation, we have unleashed the biggest monster humans have ever fought and it is far, far bigger than all the monsters we humans have faced before. It is bigger than the giant cave bears, herds of woolly mammoths, giant lions and sabre toothed tigers put together and charging all at once. This monster is the system of land ownership and land collateral for loans that the global economy has become. This monster has developed into the full blown system of usury that the financial economy has become.

Do we fight or tame this monster? The monster acts with bullying and thuggery. The opposite to bullies in my opinion are the dignified meek. It is us people, humble enough to know we are a participating part in the ever evolving organism of the Earth who are the dignified meek. I think the time has come for us meek, as one of the ancient perceptive ones has said, to be blessed and inherit the earth. One of the things the trade of husbandry teaches is that us feeble, meek and pathetic people can, with patience and skill, work with and within the hugely powerful forces of nature. We dignified meek have the power to deal with the enemies of land communities. Land communities have teaching and storytelling facilities. Land communities are the places where the arts of taking care are nurtured and learnt.

---

[22] C Clay, Lifeleasehold in the Western counties of England 1650-1750

I believe we need to set up schools, universities of learning and qualifications in husbandry all over and everywhere in this land and every inhabited land. This is a mutual learning task – information and skill sharing. This is a mutual leadership task.

Husbandry – A paradigm shift

A wild beast becomes domestic livestock by a process of taming. We teach it to take care. To do this we need tools. A stick and a carrot. A firm but gentle stick and a tasty garden-grown carrot are best.

We today are faced with this beast: the beast, once again, is the system of land ownership and land collateral for loans which the global economy has become.

What are these metaphorical tools of sticks and carrots, and how do we use them to tame this beast?

The carrot seems to me to be a vision of the world for the future prosperity of all of us who at present are participating in this cheating back-stabbing monster. This vision is a future in our world – built along lines of sharing it respectfully and with full dignity, us users of it paying full dues for our privilege. This payment of dues will be funding the facilities of community hospitality. The vision is a world available for all who wish to husband portions or wanderings of it. The vision is a world which will become, with the skills of the peoples and places of the world a complete, beautiful and respectful place to bring our children and grandchildren up in.

So that's the carrot for all of us who at present participate in keeping the monster growing. It is very, very tasty. Think of productive pleasure gardens around our homes and along our ways and byways.

And the stick – I'm afraid the stick is coming whatever any of us can do – let's use the stick carefully. The stick is very firm. The stick gives this message to the monster:

"We are not going to play with you any more. You are no longer our alpha. A debt to you is meaningless. You have been feeding off the cream and most of the skim milk of our efforts to husband the earth and our support for you is withdrawn.

You will ask us – to be paid handsomely with more debts – to take up arms to protect yourself and we will refuse. We have learned much since you called our grandfathers to the trenches in the First World War, our fathers and mothers to terrors in the second. We will not allow you a third.

You will ask us and we will refuse. We will lay down our weapons and take up our hoes. This land is our land. *We* are a big and complicated thing. *We* have many parts, each demanding dignity and claiming ever deeper levels of learned respect."

Human Cultures: Agri Cultures and Urban Cultures

So back to the scene of the sheep clipping. I'm warm and dry in a luxury coach heading back in that direction. London, with its heavy, sharpened iron spikes surrounding structures to self-importance, has given way to big beautifully ploughed fields with not a soul anywhere to be seen. The rain has stopped and the sun is starting to dry things out.

Another little bit of vision of how the future could be in this urban and rural view from my bus window: without taxes to stifle marginal improvements, with full payment of dues for use of all locations, I can see people and gardens growing out of the disused margins of these fields. I can hear laughter, music and watch dancing, culture returning to this at present barren agriculture. I can see joy and children playing around productive gardens growing from the disused margins of this big industrial city I am leaving behind.

Can we start this awakening now? Can we begin a journey together of becoming earth people? Husbanders? Agriculturas? Economy practicers? Yeomen and yo women?

Can we, right now, bring to bear all our carrots and all our sticks to taming this monster who behaves like our alpha but is no longer? Each and every culture and each and every time honoured diplomatic skill of exchange between cultures is our source of both sticks and carrots. Let's help each other in this renaissance - "an agrarian renaissance" as Colin Tudge has called it [23].

Some people might interpret this as a calling for revolution against the status quo. But the beauty of this analysis - brought forward by all those thinkers and doers previously mentioned - is that our society's laws on property tenure mechanisms do not need any upheaval - they need to be looked at carefully with fresh eyes. Husbandry clauses in tenure documents need to be researched and some respect paid to them [24]. What needs to happen is that us beneficiaries of tenure - we settlers and our fences - urban, spiked with iron or rural, need to pay our dues. Let's find out what the levels of those dues are: how many people wanting to be close to the wonderful facilities of our roads and cities, largely determines the dues to be paid for a fair deal with other settlers and wanderers. We ARE capable of making fair deals and we are capable of using dignified diplomatic hospitality. We have excellent valuation services to call upon.

The value of Abel's land with its husbandry obligations and lifetime's rewards needs to be fairly agreed with Cain so they can both lay down their weapons and have dignified conversations over the fence. There are many stories to tell. As Wendell Berry says, "It all turns on affection" [25].

Agriculture is a much misunderstood and frightening word. It comes from Latin meaning to bring culture, with all its music and laughter, as well as tools to handle the dirt, to the open spaces of the world. *Agora* - open space; *culture* -

---

[23] Colin Tudge, Good Food for Everyone Forever 2011

[24] Two Examples of husbandry clauses in land tenure documents: Liddy Ball 3 year business tenancy and 1722 Fair Oak 7 year tenancy www.husbandry.co.uk/downloads

[25] Wendell Berry, National Endowment for the Humanities 2012 Jefferson Lecture

culture and cultivate. All of us can bring whatever skills we have to wherever we habitually tread and begin a bond, paying our dues and nothing else to nobody else except by fair and friendly dealing. We can all bring our culture to the open spaces surrounding us, and begin to cultivate them. This more everyday meaning of agriculture gives us urban folk permission to be involved in agricultural acts. Wendell Berry again: "Eating is an agricultural act" [26]. With the power of urban culture involved in the business of agriculture, every human and land community has a great and wonderful future.

I believe it is time for a renaissance in husbandry; a brightening of the edge of husbandry. It is not rocket science – it is starting with the mess we have allowed to happen around us and beginning to stack it, like a dung heap, learning levels of respect and love for it as we go. I'm the worst husbander in the world – look at how many tools I leave out in the rain, I am untidy and leave maybe more mess behind me as I sort out in front – just ask my ever tolerant wife. If *I* can begin to learn to husband my very own 'we', anybody can. It is a journey which begins every day. Let's all begin today. There is a messy world all around us. This world is our world to learn to take care of. We can do this by handling the stuff it is made of. Bit by bit. It is made of dirt. Dirt is ok to handle. We can wash our hands afterwards. There's not *so* much to be afraid of.

We *are* learning from the mistakes of the Romans in neglecting their agriculture. We *are* learning from the mistakes of our grandfathers. Let's all encourage each other in applying our minds, our skills and our bodies to connecting culture and agriculture in our cities, our open spaces and all the places we inhabit. Let's all encourage each other to cultivate the places we inhabit.

In this journey through a winter, spring and summer attempting the difficult task of husbandry, I have at last come to see what husbandry is. There are a couple of Devon

---

26 Wendell Berry " The Pleasures of Eating" from What are people for? 1990

expressions that help here. One is 'Proper job', often said when a job just finished is seen to be done to a good enough level. Another is the expression 'Proper order', referring to standards of work consolidated over a long time. Husbandry is a 'Proper order' business.

It is the 'Proper order' business of being human. It is the art of taking care of all the connections that sustain us...

Husbandry is also the proper order business of agriculture – the taking care of the open spaces of the world. It involves treating the stuff to be handled with dignity and respect and over time with a growing love and intimacy.

It follows that the proper order business of being human includes agriculture. Proper order agriculture is human-scale business, and we urban humans need to take back a cultural and cultivational relationship with all those neglected open spaces with which we are surrounded. Open spaces are the places we can occupy with affection where we can process the mess we are surrounded by and, bit by bit, create productive gardens out of the bond between people and place.

A hundred years ago my grandfathers were going through difficult times answering the call that went up on posters: "Your Country Needs You". Perhaps now we can have a slightly different interpretation of what *country* means. It is the physical spaces we all occupy and need to occupy, in an agricultural manner. It is the locations, urban and rural, which not only need looking after but also have the potential of being productive of the things we humans desire. Agricultural occupation is the business of being human; it has, after a long period of apprenticeship, and a lifetime's journey, the potential of being a high art. Walter, for me, represented the Michelangelo of the profession. His masterpiece was his being true to his calling, keeping this most honourable craft alive in his bond with the land of Fair Oak. His work is his contribution to the landscape of that part of Devon and in the demonstration of the creative potential of this art. He did this through some of the most terrible and tragic times of the 20th century. His work is his contribution to the landscape of what it is to be human.

I remember Walter's father, Tom, as an old man tending his fields. When out checking his sheep, he would walk over a few fields every day, maybe taking slightly different routes each time. I remember him often taking a small mattock with him, sometimes using it as a walking stick, sometimes slicing a thistle just below the surface of the grass.

Keeping grass clear of thistles is a big deal as anyone who has looked after grassland will tell you. By this very simple multi-tasking, cutting a few thistles while tending their flocks, Tom and Walter kept two hundred and forty acres more or less clear of these unwanted weeds. So much productivity with effort used so sparingly. This is just one small example of how these skilled husbandmen lived their lives, and built the landscape they belonged to.

So rather than letting the corporations and governments send my sons off to fight more terrible wars, perhaps we should reissue the posters, saying "Your Country Needs You", and this time we all, urban and rural respond not by signing up to their wars, but with our raised beds and planters. We respond with all the cultural tools at our disposal.

We need to occupy 'waste' land. We need to occupy and nurture the land communities, with respect not only to the ecological communities, but also to the human communities which are all connected. The links that need to be made are these links between the land and human communities of the world. We must not fall into the trap of thinking we own land communities. We humans are merely a humble member of them, a husband to them. We may demand agricultural tenure of these waste places and we may demand this simply by starting to have a cultivational and cultural relationship with these places. We must not forget to ensure there are husbandry clauses in all tenancy agreements secured by our agricultural occupation of land communities. All occupation of land, which includes all urban land like the location of Selfridges, all along Oxford Street and behind those spiked railings, needs husbandry clauses. Proper order agricultural occupation of our streets and places is the main bit missing in the otherwise brave Occupy movements in cities all around the world. We urban humans need to remind ourselves that Earth communities are there to be nurtured in all environments.

By doing so, we will create new demands. Our corporations and their ability to respond to demands will need to become tamed, and serve us people with humility, providing us, I hope, and I trust, with good, smart husbandry tools. We need tools using good smart energy to help us with the task of taking care of all that stuff. Agriculture is a difficult job, it always has relied on supplementary energy provided by domestic animals, then by slavery and now by fossil fuels. Some of the big fossil fuel powered agricultural tools are very smart, but they are paid for by too high a price in the lack of intimate care they are able to take of the ecologies of the open spaces where they are used. We need human-scale smart tools now.

Husbandry is the business of people. There is a growing critical mass of people making this commitment to love and honour, for better and for worse, in sickness and in health, the places we inhabit in mother earth. I see it happening all round the world right now. It is a Proper job.

A Manifesto for Paying Due Respect and Paying Dues to the Communities of Earth

1. Earth communities belong to us humans. We belong to earth communities.

2. A mutual belonging, ourselves to the earth, the earth to ourselves, is not an owning relationship.

3. Husbandry, stewardship and agriculture are some of the arts by which we humans conduct these belonging relationships.

4. If, due to the practical requirements of settled husbandry, the belonging relationship needs to be exclusive, then full compensation to the rest of the earth communities must be paid in order to maintain proper, respectful relationships with the rest of the earth communities.

5. This compensation for an exclusive, belonging relationship represents a formal, economic and legal way of demonstrating the due respect that the husband of one earth community pays to the rest of the earth communities.

6. Paying due respect is a practical, social, economic and ethical duty. It is performed by whoever benefits from an exclusive, belonging relationship with a bounded part of the Earth, paying their dues.

7. Dues are to be paid by us humans and human-like bodies (i.e. companies, corporations and governments) to the governing authorities we people democratically authorise.

8. This paying of dues is to replace all existing methods of financing our public bodies.

9. This manifesto is a call to each and every one of us – the world over – to begin husbandlike or wifelike relationships with our earth communities. The duties of a husband – to love, to cherish, to honour – for better or for worse etc., are well known. The art of husbandry is a simple business of applying these principles to our marriages with Mother Earth.

10. This manifesto is a call to all of our governors – all of our "alphas" in every field of human endeavour – to begin to acquaint ourselves with the moral, economic and philosophical principles of husbandry.

11. This manifesto is a call to all people, in every position of power or lack of it – to begin to acquaint ourselves with the practical change in the rules of engagement that our economic system needs, so that the paying of due respect to the earth communities may flourish from now on.

12. The practical change in the rules of engagement involves a move away from outright ownership of parts of the Earth (this is slavery of earth communities) towards valuing the parts of the Earth we use and towards setting up systems which enable us all to pay our due respect and our dues.

13. This manifesto calls for us all to begin to define the ecological, land and community boundaries we are each able to be responsible for and to begin the life-giving journey of tending them and everything within them.

Boundaries of legitimacy

There is a thin thread of husbandry linking generation to generation all the way from where we are today to the earliest origins of humanity. This thread is what has kept us going through all the wars, through all our uncouth behaviour towards each other and through all the tragedies of history. The thread is sometimes poor, badly-spun and lacking substance, such as my own puny efforts, and it is sometimes well-spun, strong, yeoman-like work such as practised by my teacher Walter. Nevertheless it is a thread that still links all of humanity to our origins in the mists of Nature. What if this obscure trade, this "first and most useful of all the necessary arts" came to be practised more widely? What if it was to be practised by everyone, from busmen to bankers, from anarchists to archbishops? What if husbandry was to be practised by the strongest, the most intelligent, the generals of the military and the captains of industry?

The simple act of becoming responsible for boundaries around some sort of patch of this earth will inevitably lead to both acts of love and acts of carelessness, successes and mistakes, by all those busmen and bankers, anarchists and archbishops. These acts will, sometimes with patience and sometimes quickly, yield 'learning' – a never-ending learning of how to care for the life in and within those boundaries. What a magnificent, strong and multi-layered thing this thread will become! What a tapestry human power could weave out of this thread as a gift to our grandchildren!

A Next Stage in our Growing up and Linking-up

O.K, so now we come to our conclusion.

We have found a way to prevent a recurrence for our sons and daughters of the terrible times my grandfathers, Alfred and Arthur, and so many others went through a century ago.

We have found that land is a community that we humans are members of.

We have found that these earth communities need to have boundaries.

We have found that a proper order way of being members of land communities is by being husbands or wives to them.

We have found that earth communities are everywhere – urban and rural, waste land as well as best city land. We have discovered that we need to occupy, in a kindly and agricultural manner, all these places we find around us.

We have found that earth communities need the best of human culture; agriculture needs urban culture and vice versa.

We have found there is a fundamental conflict involved in husbandry or long term stewardship of a bounded piece of the earth. How do you compensate those kept outside the bounds? This I call the Cain and Abel conflict for short.

The systemic flaw in the planet to human relationship is the system of land ownership backed up by violence – Cain's solution.

And we have found there is a remedy to this.

We have found there is a way to align the economic forces we are all subjected to with the task of taking care of bounded parcels of our world.

Civilisation has taken land wholesale, and it has done great and terrible things with this taking. Civilisation has enslaved land. Now is the time to begin to unshackle these land communities, and set them free to begin human relationships with all people.

The remedy is the dismantling of the violence-backed system of land ownership. In its place we build a system of payment of proper dues to our larger earth communities for the exclusive use of the bounded parcels of land we settlers demand.

This payment of dues enables each of us to pay proper respect to our relationships with the pieces of land we know. The associated dismantling of taxes enables the husbands and wives of earth communities to reap the rewards of the intimate care we may give them.

Most importantly it enables us to put aside the weapons which maintain our arrogance of land ownership and to pay proper respect to the other earth communities we share this planet with.

We simply need to start to link up ourselves and the Earth communities we belong to.

And when we settle, to pay our dues.

Earth Duties

There are two sides to being a member of an earth community.

First there is husbandry: a duty of care within the community boundaries.

Second there is a duty of care to those excluded beyond the boundaries. This is achieved by means of a payment of dues for the privilege of exclusive use.

Separately these duties have mostly been ignored.

Hand in hand they will revolutionise humanity's care both for itself and for the Earth.

References

Berry, Wendell., "The Unsettling of America: Culture and Agriculture", *Sierra Club Books,* 1977

Berry, Wendell., Jefferson Lecturer 2012 " It all turns on Affection", *National Endowment for the Humanities* 2012

Berry, Wendell., "What are People for?", *North Point Press,* 1990

Berry Wendell., "Renewing Husbandry", *Crop Science,* May-June 2005

Churchill, Winston., Hansard 1909, www.landvaluetax.org/current-affairs-comment/winston-churchill-said-it-better-than-we-can.html

Clarke, Adam., "Commentary on the Bible" 1831 http://www.sacred-texts.com/bib/cmt/clarke/gen009.htm

Clay, Christopher., "Lifeleasehold in the Western Counties of England 1650-1750" *Ag. History Review,* 1981

Denman, D.R., "Origins of Ownership", *Allen and Unwin,* 1958

Dickson, Adam., "Husbandry of The Ancients" *J Dickson and G Robinson,* Edinburgh and London, 1788

Gaffney, Mason., "After the Crash: Designing a Depression Free Economy" *Wiley-Blackwell* 2009

George, Henry., "Progress and Poverty" *Wm M Hinton* San Francisco 1879

Hudson, Michael., "Mesopotamia and Classical Antiquity" *Robert Andelson* 2000

Hudson, Michael., "The Lost Traditions of Biblical Cancellations" *Henry George School of Social Science* 1993

Judeaus, Philo "On Husbandry" http://www.earlychristianwritings.com/yonge/book11.html

Leopold, Aldo., "A Sand County Almanac" *Oxford University Press* 1948

"A New English dictionary on Historical Principles - Husbandry" *Clarendon Press* 1897

Pratt, Julian., "Stewardship Economy: private property without private ownership" *Lulu* 2011

Redfearn, David., "Tolstoy: principles for a New World Order" *Shepheard-Walwyn* 1992

Shakespeare, William "The Tragedy of Hamlet, Prince of Denmark" (Polonius) 1599/1602

Smith, Adam., "An Inquiry into the Nature and the Causes of The Wealth of Nations" 1776

Tudge, Colin., "Good Food for Everyone Forever" *Pan Publishing* 2011

Set in the heart of the beautiful Devon country-side, The Husbandry School is the joint venture of Carole and Jonty Williams. A journey that started many years back, it is the passionately held culmination of both their lives. The Husbandry School has been set up as a centre of learning linking up cultures with agricultures, hospitality with horticulture, school curricula with practical land care, people with the land.

The Husbandry School –

- Provides courses, education and training.

- Explores the ideas and practice of ecologically sound land management.

- Develops the concept of twinning urban resources with rural resources.

- Devises better ways of managing land tenure, so that people with little knowledge of agriculture can gain a secure stake in the land, and in the practice of a husbandry-based business.

- Contributes to better ways of doing business and trade locally and globally so principles of economic justice can ultimately be applied worldwide.

- Produces local food for local people.

- Provides chefs with high quality local produce.

The Husbandry School, Liddy Ball, Bickington, Devon TQ12 6NZ UK

www.husbandry.co.uk

About the Henry George Society of Devon

Initiated in 2012, the Henry George Society of Devon is an informal group with a shared enthusiasm for the ideas of 19th century political economist Henry George. His central proposal is that all taxes should be removed and replaced by a charge for the use of land – the Single Tax or Land Value Tax. We feel that these ideas are essential if prosperity is to be shared by all in society. Therefore our stated aim is to foster and promote a greater understanding of Georgist economics in Devon UK. We do this by "flying the Georgist flag" and providing a point of contact, forum and support network for likeminded people in this part of the world. We also give presentations, host discussions and provide information to individuals and groups.

We believe that correctly understanding the fundamental root cause of the problem is the most vital step towards solving it. Our activities are therefore first and foremost directed at education. As George himself wrote:

> *"Until there be correct thought, there cannot be right action, and when there is correct thought, right action will follow"* (Social Problems, 1886).

Individual members undertake a variety of activities such as speaking engagements, writing books, hooking up with other groups and speaking to politicians. Our meetings, held four or five times each year, are an opportunity to share experiences, listen to guest speakers and discuss the issues of the day. These meetings are always open to newcomers who are curious to learn more. If you would like to learn about Georgist economics, would like us to give a talk or wish to join us and/or help us further our aims please get in touch by emailing henrygeorgedevon@gmail.com.

Other publications by the Henry George Society of Devon:

Julian Pratt (2014) Supporting local economies: from Business Rates to Land Value Taxation

http://henrygeorgedevon.wordpress.com